BELWIN MASTER SOLOS

TROMBONE INTERMEDIATE

GRADED SOLOS for the Developing Musician
Edited by KEITH SNELL

CONTENTS

Solo Book available separately.

Design: Odalis Soto

ORIENTATION

This book is one of three levels of trombone solos in the Belwin Master Solos series. Prepared under the direction of Keith Snell, each of these folios contains a collection of graded solos that should prove to be a useful source for both the student and the teacher of the trombone.

The solos in these folios include works from the Renaissance, Baroque and Classical periods, folk songs and traditional tunes, and a selection of original compositions for trombone.

The student will find that these solos provide material with specific challenges in rhythm, range, and key signatures in music that is both instructive and enjoyable to perform. The teacher will find these solos useful because each has been selected and arranged to challenge the student in different areas of technique and musicianship while providing exposure to a variety of musical styles.

INTERMEDIATE LEVEL - SOLOS

The solos in this folio are designed to provide the intermediate level trombone student with challenges in all areas of playing technique, including range, key signatures and complex rhythms, and in developing the technique of solo performance.

In an effort to expose the intermediate student to a cross section of musical styles, arrangements of music from the various stylistic periods have been included. In transcribing the various selections to accommodate the trombone, it has been necessary to make alterations to the original form of some of the pieces such as in key or range. However, this has permitted the use of a wider selection of music from the various historical and stylistic periods. In so doing, it is hoped that this will help the student to develop a greater understanding and appreciation for these musical styles and will encourage them to explore these styles further as their technique develops.

Two Royal Fanfares
1. Prelude to "Te Deum"

Marc-Antoine Charpentier (1634-1704)
Arranged by Keith Snell

EL03540

4

2. La Réjouissance

Georg Philipp Telemann (1682-1767)
Arranged by Keith Snell

8

Nocturne

John Tyndall

14

41

Habanera
from "Carmen"

Georges Bizet (1838-1875)
Arranged by Keith Snell

EL03540

Gigue

George F. Handel (1685-1759)
Arranged by John Tyndall

EL03540

Abendlied
(Evening Song)

Robert Schumann, Op. 85, No. 12 (1810-1856)
Arranged by Christopher Nolan

EL03540

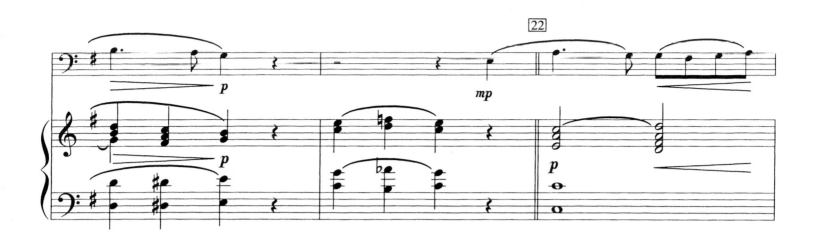

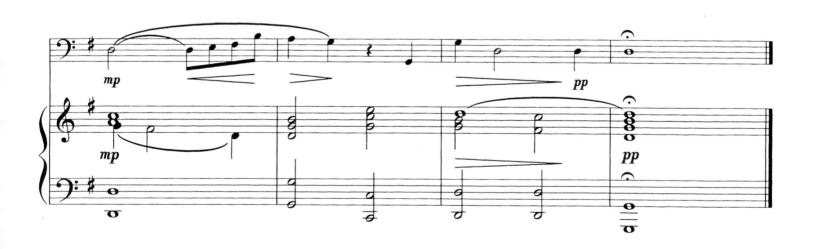

Three Miniatures
No. 1

Keith Snell

No. 2

Keith Snell

No. 3

Keith Snell